Diary Of A Spotless Mind

Poems On Love Hope Existence

Dr Ishan Choudhary

BookLeaf Publishing

India | USA | UK

Made with ❤ on the BookLeaf Publishing Platform
www.bookleafpub.in
www.bookleafpub.com

Dedication

Dedicated to my mother.

Preface

In the realm of words, where emotions ebb and flow, this collection of poems invites you to embark on a journey of self-discovery, love, and contemplation. This collection has been a journey, a quiet conversation whispered between my heart and the blank page.These poems are a reflection of the beauty and chaos that surrounds us, a testament to the resilience of the human spirit. These poems are not meant to provide answers, but rather to ask questions. As you delve into this world of words, may you find solace, inspiration, and a deeper connection to the world around you. May these poems be a reminder that, even in the darkest moments, there is always beauty to be found, and that the power of words can transform, heal, and uplift us all .

Acknowledgements

Thanks to all those people who gave a little hope to someone by being kind

Were you kind today ?

1. Away from welcome mats

Away from welcome mats
I found solace under a lonely tree
And falling autumn leaves
Where memories of my
childhood days came to play with
me
Isolated myself from civilisation
and its cruelty

Away from welcome mats
On top of mountains
I set my inner child free
My innocence kept flowing

Away from welcome mats
In lap of my mother
Finally I slept in peace

2. Story of an outcast

Rejected by society
Rejected by friends
The boy in distressed jeans
And a pony tail
Didn't care much
Sang his own song
Carried his own weirdness
Happy with himself
Lived at his own terms
Played his guitar
Wrote his own songs
The boy in distressed jeans
Listen to his own heart
Rejected by society

Rejected by friends

Didn't want much money

Didn't want much fame

Didn't want much glory

Oh really he didn't care

The boy in distressed jeans

And a pony tail

Lived like an outcast

Died like a poet

3. A walk to remember

Walking with her in the rain
With clear dark sky
Bloody moon
Wind blowing directly to our wet
faces
Road filled with thrills
of unsafe encounters
With our hearts pounding
Recalling old memories
What went wrong in the past
How could we didn't meet often
We both were clueless
May be destiny had some other
plans

May be we have to wait for
another lifetime
Trying to protect her
We walked straight
Into the dark of the night
As we reached closer to our
destination
Our hearts settled down
But few questions remain
unanswered
And we shook our hands
To say final goodbye
I turned back
Night got darker and scarier
But I was fearless , as I was
alone

As I was walking back
I knew I had just experienced the
most
Thrilling walk of my life
That will forever stays with me

4. Still in childhood

If you can retain your innocence
You are still in childhood
If you can carry some sweetness
in your heart
In this cruel world
You are still in childhood
If you can look at a girl wearing
short dress
with grace
You are still in childhood
If you can enjoy little joys of life
You are still in childhood
I think
I am still in childhood

5. Happy in my dream

Lying in your arms
Sleeping like a sloth
Making morning coffee for you
Long evening walks to nowhere
Gossiping in an ice cream
parlour
Cigarettes after sex
I am happy in my dreams
In my dreams you are still there
In my dreams we are still
together
Let me be
Let me die

In my sleep
I am happy in my dream

6. Poem by an orphan boy

Through the eyehole of my
kaleidoscope
I can see the unicorns flying
Guardian angel protecting me
I am surrounded by friends and
family
I am getting all the love that I
always needed

Through the eyehole of my
kaleidoscope
I can see myself winning the rat
race
Getting fame and money

Surrounded by beautiful girls

Through the eyehole of my
kaleidoscope
I can see my world just fine

7. What is art ?

Her eyes , Her lips

Her fingertips , Her earrings

Her voice , Her kindness

8. Ballad of Debbie Grace

Reckless sensation
Most beautiful girl of this town
With fire in her eyes
Magic in her soul
Debbie Grace
Wearing sunglasses, speeding her
Mercedes Benz
Clubbing, partying
Soaking winter sun
A courage that defies social
norms
A poets dream
Like a rainbow in a cloudy
weather

Like a shimmering light
in darkness
Debbie Grace
Breaking boys heart
Broke my heart
That's her way
Debbie Grace
A rebel
Reckless sensation
Wearing sunglasses, speeding her
Mercedes Benz
Debbie Grace
Hope
I'll see you again

9. Raining in my eyes

It's raining in my eyes
Everything is out of control
My girl left me
My brother is out of town
I am lonely with few cigarettes
With my thoughts around
Blue light in my room
Giving a sense of ugliness
With no food left to eat
I am hungry and cold
Waiting for my love to come
back soon
So we can have dinner
In dim candlelight

To take my pain away
And give me some sight
To see perfectly
That's hampered
By raining in my eyes

10. In her eyes

There's something in her eyes
That's disturbing my nights
The way she looks at me
I always lose my mind
Her purple hairs
Feels like a starry night
Scent of her perfume
Smells like a breeze of jasmine
Craving for a hug
But that's a distant possibility
Hopefully I'll see her again
And look into her eyes
To disturb my nights

11. Wild flowers

In a darkened room
I am loosing my soul
Snorting cocaine , injecting
opioid
Guilt , fear , shame engulfing
my mind
In a hopeless life still hoping that
You will come back again

To show me you still care
Send me wild flowers to give me
some hope
Send me wild flowers to ease my
pain

Send me wild flowers to show me
you are still there
or you have to put roses on my
grave

12. Sleepless road

As I lit the cigarettes
Under this lonely street light
With your memories flooding my
heart
Burning my soul
Trying to calm my nerves
With another unsuccessful
attempt
And another sleepless night

13. Letter to a friend

Dear Partha
Thanks for the kind words
You know how many inner
battles we fought
To reach here
The antidepressants
The madness
The wild nights full of alcohol ,
sadness, homesickness and
stupidity
We destroyed ourself for nothing
Then came failures , heartbreaks
suicidal thoughts

To reach here at this level
Where we are still alive
And getting atleast few hours of
sound sleep
Feels like a great victory
If only for ourselves
Finally existence showed us some
mercy
You were always there for me
Don't worry about my loyalty

Your friend
Ishan

14. ADHD Kid

Got bullied in school
Got bullied at home
Never begged for mercy
With demons in his head
The boy fought hard
No happiness no friends
A lonely fight against the world
With no place to call home
The boy carried on with
cigarettes, wine and scars on his
face
Years passed on
And that ADHD kid

Now my friend

Working as a doctor

15. River of grief

Sailing through the river of grief
It's too deep and too scary to
think
Can you come with me to river
of grief
Help me find my way through
the storm
Let's sink to the bottom of grief
Find meaning of despair and
peace
It's getting dark and frightening
tonight
Help me find a way out of
darkness of night

I am too scared and
lonely tonight
Can you come here and set me
free
I am sailing through the river of
grief

16. Paranoid

Screams in my head
Visions in corner of my eyes
Am I going insane
Or these are the sensations of a
normal man
Spiders fighting in my head
Death in the corner
Is this the road to hell
Or I am being paranoid
Looking for some help in my
delusional world
Waiting for my mama to come
To fight devil in my head

Till then I am paranoid
Till then I am paranoid

17. Chai paani café

Look at this place
Bursting with youth
Bursting with energy
Girls look good
In tight pants
In baggy jeans
Tea is flowing
Smoke in the air
There's much pain in the world
But not at this place

18. Misfits

Being a misfit in a well organised
society, never felt accepted

It felt awesome sometimes

It felt awful sometimes

But being a misfit just never
felt accepted

19. Tears of disgust

I saw an old man begging on the
streets
And kids hitting him with sticks
I stopped them
But the tears of disgust started
flowing
I saw a girl being harassed by
youth
I stopped them
And my tears of disgust kept
flowing
I saw a govt official bulldozed an
old man kiosk
I couldn't stop them

My tears of disgust kept flowing
I saw a kid selling water bottles
at railway station
I gave him 500 bucks
But the tears of disgust kept
flowing
I saw people being ugly to each
other
Saw loss of humanity
Failed to observe kindness
I saw the world turning into
monster's kingdom
And
My tears of disgust kept flowing
forever

20. No Joy

I fell in love
And you left me
I lost my happiness

I went to college drank alcohol
Fucked girls
But found no happiness

I got success
Performed surgeries
Saved life
Found no happiness

I left my job
Worked for an NGO

Worked for the outcasts
Found no happiness

I won the rat race
Made money
Found no happiness

I lived a good men life
Stayed kind
Helped everyone
Found no happiness

Finally I died
I went to heaven
Met God
Found no happiness

God sent me back to earth
I met you again
Slept in your lap
And finally I found my
happiness

21. Fading away

You are leaving me tomorrow
Good times are fading away
With you I felt happiness
My happiness is fading away

I will miss your gentleness
My gentleness is fading away

With you my spring is going
away
I am left cold and alone
My flowers are fading away

Hope you will have good life
With your love

My love is fading away

May be in parallel universe
We are still together
In this universe our togetherness
Is fading away

I always prayed for your well
being
Now my prayers are fading
away
I promise to find you in next life

Till then my life is fading away

9 789369 537716